# Arachnids ABCs

Domain Eukaryota → Kingdom Animalia → Phylum Arthr... ...bphylum
Chelicerata → Clade Dekatriata → Class Arachnida

Arachnids are:

- **invertebrates** with an **exoskeleton**, like all arthropods, as well as internal cartilage-like tissue called the **endosternite**
- almost entirely composed of organisms with **eight legs** (though some mites have 4 or 6 legs)
- organisms with **chelicerae** (mouthparts, 'jaws,' or articulated fangs similar to pincers) for feeding & defense
- organisms with **pedipalps** appendages next to the chelicerae for feeding, motion, & reproduction; some are so small that they look like chelicerae & some are so big that they look like another pair of legs
- divided into two body sections (**tagmata**)—the **cephalothorax** (front part) & the **abdomen** (back part)

Arachnids are mostly **carnivorous**. Only harvestmen & some mites eat solid food particles; other arachnids (like most spiders) digest the bodies of insects & small animals externally before eating them. Many species are **venomous**, evolved to help them kill prey or defend themselves. Arachnids have 2 kids of eyes, called **ocelli**—lateral (compound eyes) & median (simple eye). They also have sensory hairs (called **trichobothria**) covering their bodies that allow them to have a sense of touch.

Class Arachnida has 12 surviving Orders, containing spiders, scorpions, mites, ticks, and many more species. There are >100k named species & ~47k are spiders.

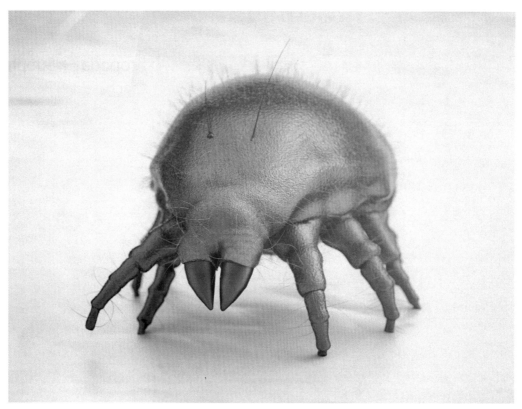

# American House Dust Mite

American House Dust Mite (or just "dust mites") are arachnids belonging to the Pyroglyphidae family. They are usually found in household dust; they feed on human & animal skin cells trapped in dust, as well as some molds. A female lives 8-10 weeks and can lay 60-100 eggs. Dust mites are a common allergen.

# Black Widow

Black Widow can refer to many species in the genus *Latrodectus*. The classic, "red hour glass" species are *L. hesperus* (southern black widow) and *L. mactans* (northern black widow). Their venom is unusually strong due to the presence of a neurotoxin called latrotoxin, which causes pain, rigid muscles, vomiting, and sweating.

# Crab Spiders

Crab Spiders are members of the Thomisidae family, and are called crab spiders because they resemble crabs—in their coloration, in how they hold up their front legs, as well as in their tendency to scuttle sideways & backwards. Instead of trapping food in a web, they are ambush predators, using their silk only for reproduction.

# Deer Tick

Deer Ticks, *Ixodes ricinus*, are hard-bodied. They are flat when they are starved, and much rounder & larger when engorged with blood. Deer ticks & other related *Ixodes* species are infamous for spreading diseases. They are the vector for spreading Lyme disease, as well as carriers for parasites and tick-borne encephalitis.

# Emperor Scorpion

The Emperor Scorpion, *Pandinus imperator*, is one of the largest scorpion species. They are popular as pets since they are fairly docile & calm. Their sting is almost harmless, and they don't use it much since they prefer to hunt and dismember their prey with their large pincers. They mostly feed on insects, but will sometimes go after small rodents.

# False Scorpions

False Scorpions are members of Order Pseudoscorpiones. They feed on ants, mites, booklice, small flies, and the larvae of various moths & beetles, so they're seen as beneficial to humans. They are extremely tiny (about 1/16th to 1/3rd of an inch), and are often mistaken for ticks or spiders. Like scorpions, their pincers are large, specialized pedipalps.

# Goldenrod Crab Spider

The Goldenrod Crab Spider, *Misumena vatia*, is named after the plant that they're most often found on—goldenrod sprays—and are in the crab spider classification since they can walk sideways & backwards. They can change color by eating certain insects (often much larger than themselves) & camp out in a single hunting ground for most of their lives.

# Harvestmen

Harvestmen, aka harvesters or daddy longlegs, belong to Order Opiliones, which has over 6,650 species. Their closest relatives are either mites or scorpions, but not spiders. Their bodies look like they only have one tagmata, but it's an illusion; the connection is just wide. They have no venom or silk glands and are ambush predators.

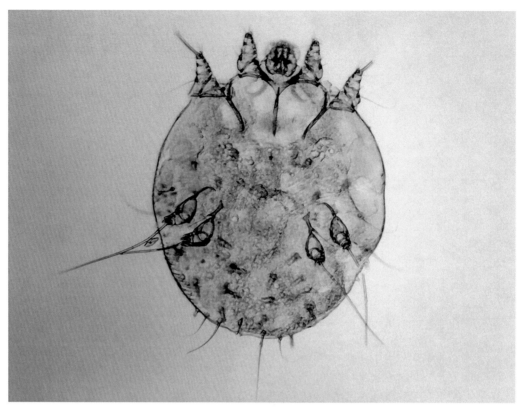

# Itch Mite

The Itch Mite, *Sarcoptes scabiei*, burrows under the skin and causes scabies. Scabies presents as severe itchiness and a pimple-like rash. Really bad scabies infections cause a scaly rash than can form a crust. Itch mites are parasitic mites that prey on humans, pets, and many other mammals; in dogs, a scabies infection is called "mange".

# Jumping Spiders

Jumping Spiders are members of the Salticidae family, which has over 6,000 species. They move slowly, but can jump really well while hunting or if startled. Jumping spiders have amazing eyesight; they all have 4 pairs of eyes, one of which is particularly large. The larger eyes are on the front of their heads, which makes hunting easier.

# King Baboon Spider

The King Baboon Spider, *Pelinobius muticus*, is a tarantula. They live in shrubs & grasses, and use them for cover for their burrows. They are one of the few spiders that use stridulation (making sound by rubbing body parts together, like grasshoppers & rattlesnakes). They rub their femurs together to make the sound to warn off predators.

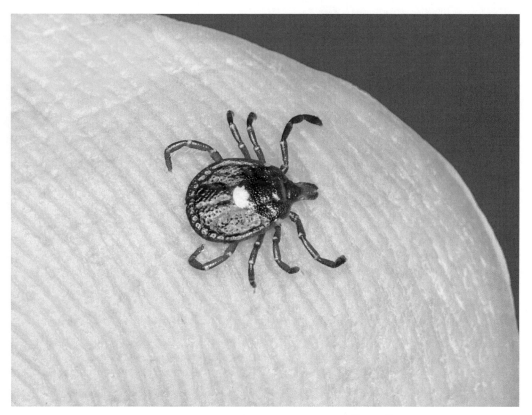

# Lone Star Tick

The Lone Star Tick, *Amblyomma americanum*, has a painless bite that usually goes unnoticed. This allows it to engorge itself on blood for up to a week. They are aggressive & attach to any host with blood. Lone Star Ticks are infamous for spreading diseases from bacteria & viruses, as well as for causing alpha-gal syndrome (allergic reaction to red meat).

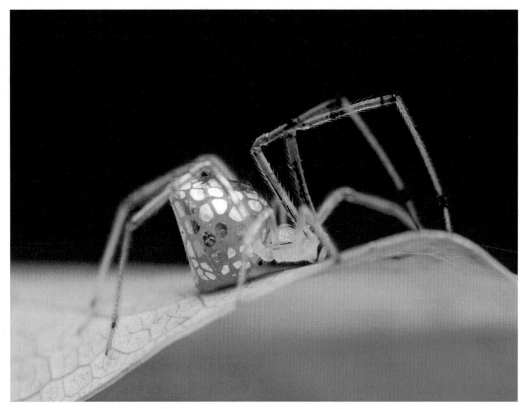

# Mirror Spiders

Mirror Spiders are all members of the genus *Thwaitesia*, also called sequined spiders. They all have patches on their abdomens which are silvery and reflective. These patches can change size if the spider feels threatened; this is done through the organic compound guanine, which is also often used by other color changing spider species.

# Naqab Desert Scorpion

The Naqab Desert Scorpion, *Leiurus quinquestriatus*, aka the Deathstalker, is one of the most dangerous scorpion species because its venom is such a lethal mix of neurotoxins. A single sting likely won't kill a healthy adult, but having risk factors or getting multiple stings can prove deadly; there is an antivenom for it, though it is not entirely effective.

# Orb-Weavers

Orb-Weavers are members of the Araneidae family and are the most common builders of spiral webs seen in gardens and forests. Their colors & patterns are diverse, but they all have eight eyes and trichobothria on their legs. They catch insects in their sticky webs, bite to stun, and wrap them in silk. They often eat the whole web (with the prey) every night.

# **Palpimanoids**

Palpimanoids are also known as assassin spiders. Many of them specialize in hunting other spiders. Some of them have long chelicerae or enlarged front legs or pedipalps to make it easier to hunt. Some species go into other spiders' webs and drag them away, while others wait for prey to run by them before snapping their jaws closed to trap them.

# Queensland Whistling Tarantula

The Queensland Whistling Tarantula, *Selenocosmia crassipes*, is another spider that uses stridulation to warn away predators, using the bristles on its chelicerae to make a hissing sound. Its venom isn't fatal to humans, but can make you sick for hours. They are sometimes called 'bird-eating' but they mostly eat insects, other spiders, & small lizards.

# Rocky Mountain Wood Tick

The Rocky Mountain Wood Tick, *Dermacentor andersoni*, feeds on any mammal. They are infamous for spreading the virus that causes Colorado Tick Fever (flu-like symptoms for ~10 days), as well the bacteria that cause Rocky Mountain Spotted Fever (flu-like symptoms, spotted rash, & possible permanent disabilities) & Tularemia (fever & skin ulcers).

# Sun Spiders

Sun Spiders, aka Camel Spiders or Wind Scorpions, belong to Order Solifugae, but they aren't true scorpions or spiders. They mostly live in dry climates, and eat arthropods & small animals opportunistically (as they happen come across them). Their chelicerae are large & form a pincer, and their front "legs" are massive pedipals for hunting & fighting.

# Tailless Whip Scorpions

Tailless Whip Scorpions, aka Whip Spiders, belong to Order Amblypygi and do not have silk glands or venomous fangs. They mostly prefer warm & humid habitats, and shelter under leaves or in caves. Their large pedipalps look like front legs, but help them grab prey, and their actual front legs are thin "whips" used as sensory organs, not for walking.

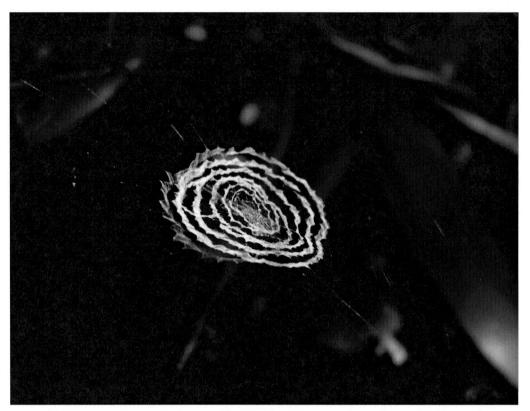

# Ulobridae Hackled Orb Weavers

The Ulobridae Hackled Orb Weavers are in a different group of spiders than the Orb-Weaver Spiders. Their webs look very similar, but they have a different kind of silk. Ulobridae silk, called hackled silk, is feathery & fuzzy. Their webs are not sticky, but the fibers form a "net" to trap prey. They wrap the prey, digest it in the silk, and eat the liquified remains.

# Vinegaroons

Vinegaroons, aka Whip Scorpions, belong to Order Thelyphonida. Their tails are thin like whips, and they attack with a liquid containing acetic acid, which smells like vinegar. Like scorpions, they have large pedipalp pincers. Like Tailless Whip Scorpions, their front legs are thin & used as sensory organs, not for walking. They eat many 'pest' bugs.

# Wolf Spiders

Wolf Spiders are members of the Lycosidae family. They have good eyesight, are good hunters, and live alone in small crevices instead of webs. Some are opportunistic hunters & some are ambush hunters. They carry their eggs at the base of the abdomen, and hatchlings ride around on top of the abdomen for several weeks before going off on their own.

# Xenesthis

*Xenesthis* is a genus of tarantulas, most known for *X. immanis* —the Colombian Lesser Black Tarantula. They are large, about 2.5 inches wide by 8 inches long, and have shown a mutualistic relationship with the Dotted Humming Frog. The tarantula protects the frog from predators and provides it with food. The frog protects the tarantula eggs from ants.

# Yellow Fattail Scorpion

The Yellow Fattail Scorpion, *Androctonus australis*, is a hardy desert species. Unlike most other desert species, they don't dig burrows to protect themselves from the environment; they are unaffected by the heat and can withstand sandstorms powerful enough to strip paint off steel. It has a potent venom made of neuro-, cardio-, myo-, & hemotoxins.

# Zebra Spider

The Zebra Spider, *Salticus scenicus*, is a common species of jumping spider. They are named for their stark black & white coloring. Their center & side eyes up front are huge compared to their four other eyes, giving them excellent vision. They mostly hunt smaller spiders & insects, but have been seen eating insects much larger than themselves.

Made in United States
North Haven, CT
30 April 2023

36067379R00015